About the Bible

Les Miller

NOVALIS

© 2012 Novalis Publishing Inc.

Cover design: Mardigrafe
Cover illustration: Anna Payne-Krzyzanowski
Interior images: pp. 8, 10, 31: Jupiter Images; pp. 17, 20, 28, 35, 39, 42, 45: Plaisted; p. 22: Eyewire
Layout: Mardigrafe and Audrey Wells

Published by Novalis

Publishing Office
10 Lower Spadina Avenue, Suite 400
Toronto, Ontario, Canada
M5V 2Z2

Head Office
4475 Frontenac Street
Montréal, Québec, Canada
H2H 2S2
www.novalis.ca

Cataloguing in Publication is available from Library and Archives Canada.

All rights reserved. No part of this publication may be reproduced, stored in a retrieval system, or transmitted in any form, or by any means, electronic, mechanical, photocopying, recording, or otherwise, without the written permission of the publisher.

We acknowledge the financial support of the Government of Canada through the Canada Book Fund for business development activities.

5 4 3 2 1   16 15 14 13 12

TABLE OF CONTENTS

A WORD FROM THE AUTHOR 5

BACKGROUND ON THE BIBLE 6

1. What is the Bible? 6
2. When was the Bible written, and who wrote it? 7
3. Who decided what to put in the Bible? 9
4. Where was the Bible written? 9
5. Why was the Bible written? 11
6. How do I find passages in the Bible? 12
7. How do we know the Bible is true? 13
8. What do things that happened so long ago have to do with me today? 15

THE OLD TESTAMENT 16

9. Was the world really created in seven days? 16
10. Why is Abraham a key biblical figure? 18
11. Who are some great women of the Bible? 19
12. Why is the story of Moses and Exodus central to our faith? 21
13. Who was King David? 24
14. What was the role of the prophets? 25

THE NEW TESTAMENT 27

15. Why do we have four Gospels to tell the story of Jesus? 27
16. What does the Bible tell us about the birth of Jesus? 29
17. What is the Kingdom of God? 31
18. How did Jesus teach about the Kingdom of God? 32
19. Why is the Last Supper important? 34
20. Why did the authorities crucify Jesus? 36
21. What happened on the first Easter? 38
22. What happened at Pentecost? 40
23. How did the early Church continue the work of Jesus? 41
24. How did St. Paul influence Christianity? 43
25. What is the Book of Revelation? 44

WORDS TO KNOW 46

25 Questions... About the Bible

A Word from the Author

This book invites you to explore the Bible more deeply. When we read the Bible, we are very close to God, because we are reading about how God guided and spoke to God's people. People who lived long ago dealt with many of the same issues we face today: How can I be happy? What is love? Why am I alive? What gives our lives meaning? Through the Bible, God still speaks to each one of us today.

My hope is that this book will lead you deeper into the wonder, wisdom and mystery that fill the Bible. The Bible contains epic stories such as the creation of the earth, the Israelites' escape from Egypt, the life of Christ, and the birth of the Church. But you will also find passages about family problems, prayers, wisdom sayings and even love poems. It's no wonder the Bible has been called "The greatest story ever told"!

I wrote much of this text while on a trip to England to celebrate my grandmother's 100th birthday. She has been an inspiration and example of loving service to our whole family all our lives. I dedicate this book to her.

Les Miller

BACKGROUND ON THE BIBLE

1

What is the Bible?

For over a thousand years, people long ago wrote down their faith stories, laws, sacred songs, letters and the Gospels. In time, all these writings, which tell the story of God's relationship with us, came to be known as the Bible.

The word "Bible" comes from the Greek word *biblia,* which means "books." Many of the writings of the Bible were written on papyrus or clay tablets. (Papyrus was an older version of paper, made from papyrus plants instead of trees.) The name makes sense, because the Bible is a collection of books.

The Christian Bible contains the Old Testament and the New Testament. The Old Testament is the Scriptures of the Jewish people. The New Testament contains the four Gospels, the Acts of the Apostles, a number of letters from leaders in the early Church to Christian communities, and the Book of Revelation. We will look at these different writings later in this book.

The word "testament" means "covenant." A covenant is a sacred agreement. Many times in the Bible we hear God say, "I will be your God and you will be my people." The people agreed to put their trust in God and to follow God's laws.

> Jewish people call their Scriptures the **Tanakh**, after the Hebrew initials for the three main sections: the Torah (Law), Nevi'im (Prophets), and Ketuvim (Writings).

❓ 2 ❓

When was the Bible written, and who wrote it?

The Bible was created over many centuries. Most of it was written between 1,000 years before the birth of Jesus until 80 years after his death and resurrection.

Some books took a long time to complete. They started as oral stories that were passed down from one generation to the next. Since most people of that time couldn't read, telling sacred stories met their needs.

After many Jewish people were forced out of the **Holy Land,** the need to write their stories became even more important. They were afraid that their children would forget the story of their relationship with God. Not only did they write down their stories, they also taught their children to read. This made the Jewish people among the most educated people at that time and for centuries to come.

25 Questions... About the Bible

Scripture scholars tell us that the earliest book of the Christian Scriptures was written around 51 AD. It is St. Paul's first letter to the Thessalonians – the Christians living in the Greek city of Thessalonica. You can find it in the Bible under the title 1 Thessalonians. The other Christian Scriptures were written over the next 60 years.

We don't know for sure who wrote many of the Bible texts. Just because a book of the Bible is named after a person, it doesn't always mean that they wrote it. For example, *Joshua* and *Job* were named after the central characters in these accounts, but they weren't the authors. In many cases, these stories had been told again and again over many years. **Scribes** would write the stories down so they wouldn't be lost. Although we don't know the names of many of the authors, Christians believe that God's Spirit flows through their words. In other words, we believe the Bible is **inspired** by God.

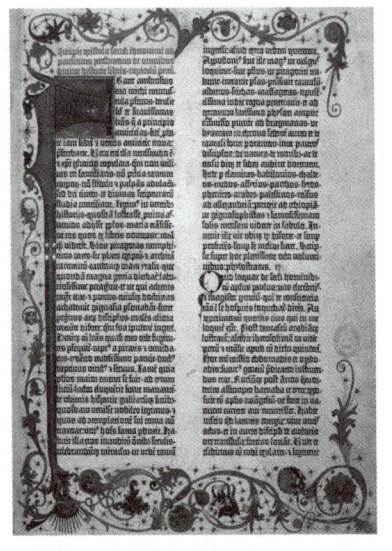

A PAGE FROM THE GUTENBERG BIBLE, THE FIRST MAJOR BOOK PRINTED (IN 1455) ON A PRINTING PRESS. UNTIL THEN, BIBLES WERE COPIED BY HAND.

25 Questions... About the Bible

3

Who decided what to put in the Bible?

Leaders of the Jewish and Christian communities decided over many years whether each "book" was truly inspired by God and worthy of being included in the Bible. For example, there were dozens of Gospels written, but the early Church leaders found that only four were worthy of becoming part of the Bible. This final decision happened at a Church council nearly 400 years after Jesus was born. The books that were included in the Bible were used widely in the study and worship of the different church communities. They contained important parts of God's saving story.

> Jewish authorities decided what to include in the Tanakh (Old Testament) during a series of meetings between 400 BC and 100 AD.

4

Where was the Bible written?

The Bible was mainly written in the Holy Land and in nearby countries. The Holy Land has been known by

25 Questions... About the Bible

many names through history, including Canaan, Israel and Palestine. Most books of the Bible were also written Egypt, Babylon (now Iraq), Syria, Turkey and Greece.

Most of the Bible was written in Hebrew and Greek. The people of ancient Israel mainly spoke Hebrew, while by the time of Jesus, people in the Holy Land spoke Aramaic. Some of the more educated people also spoke Greek (the most common language in that part of the world at that time) or Latin (the language of the Romans, the rulers at the time of Jesus). Later books of the Old Testament and all of the New Testament were written in Greek.

HERE IS AN EXAMPLE OF HEBREW WRITING.

> Hebrew is written from right to left, starting at the top of the page. The Hebrew letters are often called the "Alefbet," because the first two letters are Alef and Beit. In ancient Hebrew, the vowels were not included.

25 Questions... About the Bible

Why was the Bible written?

The Bible connects us with God. It tells the story of how much God loves us. In the Bible, we read of the different ways God offers to lead us to holiness. The Christian Scriptures, found in the New Testament, teach us that Jesus, as the Son of God, brought us into a deep relationship of love with his Father.

The Bible also teaches us how to live. We see great examples of virtue: Abraham's faith, Moses' wisdom, Ruth's love, David's courage, Mary's humility, and Paul's dedication. We find teachings about good moral choices in the Ten Commandments and in the **Beatitudes**. Because it offers guidelines for living and examples of good behaviour, the Bible can be seen as a guide to happiness.

The Bible gives us words for praise and thanksgiving. Some parts of the Bible, such as the Psalms, were written to be used in worship. We still pray and sing the Psalms at Mass today. We also reflect on the wisdom of God's word at other moments during Mass. The **lectionary** contains passages from the Bible and is treated with great reverence. That is because God is present in the Word.

The Bible also unifies people of faith. Muslims (followers of the religion of Islam) greatly respect such figures as Abraham, Moses, David, Mary and Jesus. Christians and Jews both revere the books of the Old Testament. Protestant, Orthodox and Roman Catholic Christians share almost identical versions of the Bible.

> There are 73 books in the Catholic Bible: 46 in the Old Testament and 27 in the New Testament. The Protestant Bible contains 66 books: 39 in the Old Testament and 27 in the New Testament. Protestant bibles include only those Old Testament books that the Jewish tradition recognized. Catholics and Orthodox Christians recognize seven other books that were in use in the early years of the Church.

6

How do I find passages in the Bible?

It's easier than you might think! Each passage has a kind of code. Let's use Matthew 5:3 as an example. The first part of the code is the name of the book of the Bible. In this case, it is Matthew (this is one of the four Gospels). Sometimes a short form is used instead. The short form of Matthew is Mt. You can find a table of abbreviations in the first few pages of most bibles.

25 Questions... About the Bible

Next, the book is divided into sections, called chapters, and smaller units, called verses. These chapters and verses were added between 500 and 800 years ago, making it much easier to find passages.

The first number you will see is for the chapter. In Matthew 5:3, the chapter is 5. The last number represents the verses. Verses are just one or two sentences long. In Matthew 5:3, the verse is 3. When you look up this passage in the Bible, you will find these words of Jesus: "Blessed are the poor in spirit, for theirs is the kingdom of heaven." (Your Bible may have slightly different wording: there are different ways of translating this passage from the original Greek, but the meaning is similar.)

> If you think finding your way around the Bible is difficult, have some sympathy for those who tried to read the Bible in the first few centuries after it was compiled. Putting spaces between words didn't start until around 1000 AD.

7

How do we know the Bible is true?

The Bible contains some amazing stories. We read about the creation of the world in seven days and about God parting the sea to let the Israelites escape from Egypt. Later we read about the birth, death and resurrection of Jesus. How do we know that these events really happened?

Like many things in our complex world, the answer is not simple. In fact, many of the wisest and holiest people in history have tried to answer this question. But it's not like solving a math problem. Through our belief in God, we trust and believe God's Word in the Bible.

Sometimes God's truth is hard to explain in words. Can you easily explain how your parents love you? You can give examples of how you know they love you, but you can't fully describe the mystery of love in words.

Biblical writings can give us a sense of deep wisdom and truth. Faith stories and poetry can move our minds and hearts. This form of writing is often better than direct explanations to share with us an important truth.

The Bible does use facts and history to show how God works in the world. Almost all historians agree that a person called Jesus did live in Palestine and was a wise teacher. Through the gift of faith, Christians believe that Jesus is divine.

What do things that happened so long ago have to do with me today?

The Bible was written thousands of years ago, before TV or Internet, advanced medicine or electricity, global warming or mass transit. Sometimes it may seem that the Bible has no connection to us in the 21st century.

Yet the Bible is still a central part of our lives as Christians. Why? Because it is about relationships. It certainly helps us connect with God. It also helps us deepen and improve our relations with others and the most sacred part of ourselves. The Bible even explores how we should relate with nature and the environment, which is a major issue in our beautiful but fragile world today.

The most important thing about our lives is our relationships. The Bible helps us to figure out which relationships are good and life-giving and which ones lead to selfishness and sadness. Again and again, God pleads with the people of Israel not to worship idols or false gods. When we read these passages, we can think about our own "false gods," such as celebrities or the latest fad or gadget. Do our relationships with these things interfere with our relationship with God?

25 Questions... About the Bible

For centuries, people around the world have turned to the sacred wisdom of the Bible. More copies of the Bible have been printed than any other book. We can turn to it every day to find inspiration and joy in life. Its wonderful stories, psalms and great wisdom have helped many people live happy and holy lives.

> It is a good idea to read the Bible on your own. Find a copy at a bookstore or look for apps that can give you passages to read. After a few months or years, you may have read the whole Bible! As you read, keep a journal or blog to record your thoughts, questions and favourite passages.

THE OLD TESTAMENT

9

Was the world really created in seven days?

In the Book of Genesis, the first book of the Bible, we read that God created the world in six days and rested on the seventh. Most scientists agree that the earth is about 4.7

billion years old, and during that time has been changing and producing more and more complex life. So which account is correct?

The Church teaches that both versions are true, but in different ways. The writers of the Book of Genesis did not have the scientific knowledge that we have today, and they would not have used it even if they had had that information. Instead, they used stories and imagination to help people understand the beginnings of God's love for creation, particularly human beings.

When we speak of the things that are most important to us, we don't use scientific language. For example, my grandmother just turned 100. We gathered to say, "Happy Birthday, Grandma!" No one said, "Congratulations on surviving 36,525 axial rotations of the third planet from the sun (in Earth days) and having 35 billion cardiac pulsations

"*GOD SAW EVERYTHING THAT HE HAD MADE, AND INDEED, IT WAS VERY GOOD.*" (GENESIS 1:31)

25 Questions... About the Bible

(heartbeats)!" When it comes to important relationships or events, we use the language of love.

The number seven was very important to wise people of the Bible and the Church. Seven meant sacred or perfect. Not only do we have seven days of creation, we also have seven pillars of wisdom, seven gifts of the Holy Spirit and seven sacraments. These all connect us with God in a special way. By telling us that the world was created in seven days, the writers were telling us that God created the world and time. It was a special blessing to all of creation.

Why is Abraham a key biblical figure?

The Book of Genesis tells us the story of Abraham and Sarah. They probably grew up in what is now Iraq and then settled in Canaan (now Israel). Abraham owned flocks of sheep and goats. God loved Abraham and promised to care for him and his descendants. Abraham promised to worship and obey God. This agreement is called a **covenant**.

As time passed, Sarah was sad because she couldn't have children. She asked her maid, Hagar, to have a child with Abraham: their son was named Ishmael. Then Sarah became jealous of Hagar and Ishmael, so Abraham sent them away

25 Questions... About the Bible

into the desert. According to **Muslim** tradition, Hagar and Ishmael were dying of thirst until Hagar found a well in what became the holy city of **Mecca**. Ishmael became the father of Islam, the Muslim faith.

Later, Sarah and Abraham had a son of their own, called Isaac. Abraham's faith in God was put to a great test. He was asked to sacrifice Isaac to God. At the last minute, an angel sent by God stopped the sacrifice. God knew that Abraham had great faith and no longer needed this sacrifice.

Abraham is important to Jews because his family eventually became the Israelites. Jewish people are descendants of Abraham. Christians also have great respect for Abraham, who loved God and did God's will. Muslims believe that Abraham helped to make Mecca a major place of worship for them. Jews, Christians and Muslims share Abraham as their ancestor in faith.

11

Who are some great women of the Bible?

Women have key roles in the Bible. Eve is the first woman mentioned. She is a model of the human condition: created and loved by God, yet, along with Adam, easily tempted to disregard God's will. Sarah and Hagar played an important part in Abraham's story; Rebecca, the wife of Abraham's son Isaac, advises her son Jacob on how to gain his father's inheritance.

Ruth's story is a family portrait of a woman who shows her loving-kindness in her relationships with her mother-in-law, Naomi, and her second husband, Boaz. An entire book of the Bible is devoted to Ruth's story.

Later in the Bible, you will read about the importance of Mary, the mother of Jesus. Many of Jesus' friends and follow-

JESUS VISITS THE HOME OF HIS FRIENDS MARTHA, MARY AND LAZARUS.

ers were women. Mary and Martha, the sisters of Lazarus, welcome Jesus to their home (Luke 10:38-42). Other incidents that include women are the story of the Samaritan woman in John's Gospel (chapter 4); the women at the cross as Jesus is being crucified (John 19:25-27); and Mary Magdalene, who is the first witness to Jesus' resurrection (John 20:1-9).

> Many cultures at the time the Bible was written valued men over women. The heads of families, tribes and nations were almost always male. This type of social organization is called a **patriarchy**.

???????? **12** ????????????

Why is the story of Moses and the Exodus central to our faith?

Moses was the son of **Israelite** slaves. He was raised in the Egyptian court after his mother put him in a basket when he was a baby and left him for the princess to discover. After learning of his true identity and then seeing an Israelite slave being treated brutally by an Egyptian, Moses killed the Egyptian and escaped into the wilderness. While tending his flocks, he encountered God calling to him from a burning bush. God told him to convince the Egyptians

25 Questions... About the Bible

to let the Israelite slaves go so they could return to Canaan, the **Promised Land**.

With his brother, Aaron, Moses eventually got the Egyptian Pharaoh (king) to agree (with the help of ten plagues) to God's plan. Moses led the Egyptians to the Sinai desert by parting the waters of the Red Sea so they could walk on dry land. At the last minute, Pharaoh changed his mind and the chase was on. The Egyptians tried to follow the Israelites through the sea, but as soon as God's people made it to the other side, the water came rushing back and the Egyptian soldiers were drowned.

MOSES LEADS THE ISRAELITES TO FREEDOM AS THEY ESCAPE SLAVERY IN EGYPT.

For 40 years, Moses led the Israelites in the Sinai desert until at last they reached the Promised Land. During this time, the Israelites slowly learned what it means to be a community of God's people. God gave them the Ten Commandments and many other laws to guide them in setting up their community. According to Jewish tradition, Moses also gave the people of Israel the first five books of the Bible, called the **Torah** (which means "instruction").

The story of the Israelites' escape is called the **Exodus**. Jewish people remember this important event every year when they celebrate Pesach, or Passover. The Exodus experience was a struggle for freedom. Many people today are still looking for freedom: child soldiers, child labourers, those who live in poverty, and many more. The Exodus story teaches us that God wants people to be free, and that all of us have a role to play in making freedom happen for those who are enslaved in some way.

- Moses died before he could enter the Promised Land. Joshua led the people into Canaan at Jericho.

- Jewish people celebrate the Exodus in a feast held every March or April called Passover. Jesus and his followers were celebrating a Passover meal at the Last Supper.

- Many Bible scholars believe that the Israelites crossed through a saltwater lake (the Sea of Reeds) rather than the deeper Red Sea.

Who was King David?

The Israelites settled in the land of Canaan. At first, people called **judges** provided leadership. A few centuries later, a king was chosen to lead them. The first was King Saul. They faced many enemies, including the Canaanites and the **Philistines**. During one battle, a young shepherd boy from Bethlehem named David defeated the champion of the Philistines, Goliath, using only a slingshot.

David grew so popular that King Saul became jealous. David, despite conflict with Saul, became the second king of Israel. David set up Jerusalem as his new capital city. He brought the Ark of the Covenant, which contained the tablets of the Ten Commandments, into Jerusalem. Later, his son Solomon would become king; he built a temple in Jerusalem to house the Ark.

David was known as a great leader who helped Israel to become recognized as a nation. He was also a fine musician. According to Jewish tradition, King David wrote many of the psalms we find in the Bible. But David had his weaknesses, too. He fell in love with Bathsheba, the wife of one of his soldiers. He arranged for Bathsheba's husband to be put at the front lines of battle, where he was likely to be killed. After the man died in battle, David married Bathsheba. Like many people in the Bible, David was an imperfect servant, but God never stopped loving him.

> Joseph, the husband of Mary, was a descendent of King David. His family's home was in Bethlehem. That is why Joseph and Mary had to travel to that city for the Roman census around the time of Jesus' birth.

14

What was the role of the prophets?

King Solomon was the son of David and Bathsheba and the last king of a united Israel. Fifty years after his reign, two prophets began their ministry. Elijah and Elisha were outspoken critics of those who were not living according to God's laws. They also fiercely defended Israel from rival powers that challenged their faith. Elijah, Elisha and other prophets warned that wandering from the covenant would lead to disaster. After Solomon's reign, Israel had divided into northern and southern kingdoms. The Assyrian Empire defeated the northern kingdom, called Israel, in 722 BC. It never recovered from that loss. The southern part of the kingdom, called Judah, which included Jerusalem, was later dominated by Egyptians, Babylonians, Greeks, Romans and others.

Prophets were messengers of God. With great courage and faith, they reminded their leaders and the people about their relationship with God. They used strong language and powerful examples to teach people about their responsibilities to God and to the community. Prophets demanded that the wealthy protect the poor, the widows and the orphans. Often the strong voices of the prophets brought them into conflict with the powerful. Some prophets were imprisoned or even killed. But other prophets continued to speak out.

Jerusalem was captured by the Babylonians six centuries before Jesus was born. The leaders were taken to Babylon for many years. A new role for God's messengers emerged as prophets such as Isaiah began to offer messages of hope and comfort for the **exiles**. Jesus and his cousin John the Baptist kept alive many of the themes of the prophets in their teaching, centuries later.

Here are three well-known prophets:

- Isaiah, who urged the people of Judah to repent from their sins (Jesus quoted him in the Gospels)
- Jeremiah, who was a young boy when God called him to serve God (God works through young people, too!)
- Jonah, who tried to escape his calling as a prophet but ended up being swallowed by a big fish, which then brought him to the city where he was to tell the people to turn back to God

THE NEW TESTAMENT

15

Why do we have four Gospels to tell the story of Jesus?

The Gospels of Matthew, Mark, Luke and John all tell us about the good news of Jesus Christ. When the early Christians were trying to decide which books to include in the Bible, they had many choices, because different Christian communities had different versions of the story of Jesus. The early Church leaders had to decide which accounts expressed the Christian message best. Their choice was difficult because there was some important writing in many of them. In time, they chose the Gospels of Matthew, Mark, Luke and John because they believed these were inspired by God.

The Gospels may contain the same overall message, but their approaches are slightly different. Matthew's Gospel was written for a Jewish-Christian audience around 85 AD, about 50 years after Jesus died. It shows Jesus in a Jewish setting and includes many references to the Old Testament. Mark's Gospel (the earliest Gospel, written for Gentiles and Jews in about 66 to 72 AD) is the shortest, and its writing is the most compact. Luke, who was writing for Christians in various countries around 85 AD, includes explanations

25 Questions... About the Bible

about Jewish practices. John's Gospel (written for Jewish Christians in about 95 AD) has fewer stories but longer explanations. It stresses Jesus' glory rather than his suffering.

Having four different Gospels gives us a fuller portrait of Jesus and his teaching. The main events of his life are all included: his baptism; the call of the disciples; teachings, miracles and healings; the Last Supper; his arrest, trial and crucifixion; and his resurrection from the dead. Here are some interesting facts about the Gospels:

JESUS TAUGHT HIS DISCIPLES ABOUT GOD AND HOW TO SHARE THE GOOD NEWS OF GOD'S LOVE WITH OTHERS.

- Only in Matthew's Gospel do we find the Sermon on the Mount (chapters 5 to 7).
- Only in Mark's Gospel do we read about the young man witnessing the arrest of Jesus (Mark 14:51-52).
- Only in Luke's Gospel do we find the parables of the Good Samaritan and the Prodigal Son (Luke 10:25-37 and 15:11-32).

25 Questions... About the Bible

- Only in John's Gospel do we find the story of the woman at the well (John 4:1-42).

> The Gospels of Matthew, Mark and Luke have so many things in common, they are called the "synoptic Gospels," from two Greek words meaning "from a similar point of view."

- The four Gospels were written in Greek, and have been translated into hundreds of languages, including Inuktitut and Cree.

16

What does the Bible tell us about the birth of Jesus?

We get all our information about the birth of Jesus from Matthew's and Luke's Gospels. Mark and John do not include information about this event. Luke and Matthew both focus on the birth of Jesus in Bethlehem, but they bring out different details.

Matthew stresses the role of Joseph in the **nativity** story. Before the birth of Jesus, Joseph has a dream that convinces him to marry Mary and care for Jesus. The details about the magi, Herod's jealousy, the massacre of the first-born males and the escape to Egypt are found only in Matthew's Gospel.

Luke focuses on the role of Mary. His Gospel includes Gabriel's message to Mary (the **Annunciation**), Mary's visit to her cousin Elizabeth (the **Visitation**), Mary and Joseph's journey to Bethlehem, Jesus being placed in a manger, and the visit of the shepherds and angels. It also describes Jewish birth rituals.

Both stories stress the humble, human origins of Jesus' birth in a dangerous situation. They describe the role of the wise men, or magi, who were the first to worship Jesus, and King Herod, who wanted to kill this new king. Both accounts describe Jesus as a very special person – the Messiah, or Saviour. Details about angels, stars and visions help us to understand that in the birth of Jesus, God became one of us.

> Were there *three* magi at the nativity? We don't know. The Gospel of Matthew mentions only that there were gifts of gold, frankincense and myrrh. People assumed that three gifts meant three gift-bearers, but the Bible doesn't give the names or the number of magi who worshipped Jesus at the manger.

> Bethlehem lies only 8 kilometres from Jerusalem. Today, Jerusalem is in the country of Israel, while Bethlehem is part of the Palestinian Authority. The border between the two is heavily guarded by military forces and a high wall.

What is the Kingdom of God?

The Kingdom of God was at the heart of the teachings of Jesus. In the Our Father, which Jesus taught the disciples, we pray to God, "your kingdom come." In Mark's Gospel, Jesus tells us that the Kingdom of God is near (Mark 1:15). What kind of kingdom is this?

IN THE PARABLE OF THE SOWER (MARK 4:3-9), JESUS SPEAKS OF WHAT HAPPENS WHEN THE SEED FALLS ON ROCK, OR IS CHOKED BY THORNS, OR FALLS ON GOOD SOIL. AS CHRISTIANS, WE TRY TO BE "GOOD SOIL," WHERE GOD'S WORD, THE SEED, CAN GROW IN US AND GIVE LIFE TO OTHERS.

25 Questions... About the Bible

Jesus teaches us that God's reign is one of "justice, love, and peace" (*Catechism of the Catholic Church*, #2046). Justice means treating others fairly. Jesus tells us to love God and also to "love one another as I have loved you" (John 15:12). Peace is more than the absence of conflict: it is being one with God and with our community. Peace also means forgiving others. Forgiveness is more than apologizing. It allows us to change and to heal our relationships with other people and God when they are damaged in some way.

Jesus announced that the reign of God had begun, but was not yet complete. We are still not as just, loving or peaceful as we could be. With the guidance of the Holy Spirit, the Church works to make God's reign a reality.

In Matthew's Gospel, the Kingdom of God is often called the Kingdom of Heaven.

How did Jesus teach about the Kingdom of God?

Jesus shared the important message about the Kingdom of God through his preaching, stories, prayers and actions. He describes the Kingdom of God in the Sermon on the

Mount (Matthew, chapters 5 to 7). This preaching includes the **Beatitudes**, the Golden Rule ("In everything do to others as you would have them do to you"), and the Our Father. Jesus explains how people should live in loving relationships with one another under God's guidance.

Jesus also used stories, especially **parables,** to explain the reign of God. Parables use everyday situations to reveal different aspects of the Kingdom of God. For example, Jesus uses a family dispute to teach about God's love and forgiveness in the Parable of the Prodigal Son (Luke 15:11-32).

Jesus didn't just talk about God's healing and justice. He used his power to show people that God was active among them. The miracles of Jesus are not just stories about physical healing, but are also stories about helping people to see, hear and feel God's presence around them. For example, when Jesus heals blind Bartimaeus (Mark 10:46-52), the miracle not only allows him to see, but also leads him to deeper faith in God.

Jesus taught us about being citizens of the Kingdom of God. As good citizens, we allow ourselves to let God rule our lives, even though it might be difficult at times. In the way he faced his death, Jesus showed us the courage we need. He knew he would be crucified, but he faced his last hours with dignity and trust in God his Father.

> Parables make up about one third of the Gospels of Matthew, Mark and Luke. Some well-known parables are The Parable of

25 Questions... About the Bible

the Good Samaritan, The Parable of the Lost Sheep, and The Parable of the Sower and the Seed.

????????? **19** ?????????

Why is the Last Supper important?

A week before his crucifixion, Jesus led his disciples into the great city of Jerusalem. This was the time of the Jewish feast of Passover, which recalls how God freed the Israelites from slavery in Egypt. (See Question 12.) On Thursday evening, Jesus and his disciples gathered to share a meal together. This became known as the Last Supper, because it was their final meal together.

In those days, it was the custom for servants to wash the feet of the guests before they ate. As the Last Supper began, the Gospel of John tells us, something unusual happened. Jesus, who was the leader, took over the role of the servant. He washed the feet of the disciples, even though Peter didn't want him to. Jesus told his disciples that they would also have to be servants of their communities if they were to lead in the way Jesus led people.

During the Last Supper, Jesus showed the disciples how he would remain present with them after he died, rose and ascended into heaven. He took some bread and then blessed it. He broke the bread and gave it to them to eat, saying, "Take, eat; this is my body." Then he took a cup of wine and said, "Drink from it, all of you; for this is my blood of the covenant, which is poured out for many for the forgiveness of sins" (Matthew 26:27-28). Jesus was saying that he would be present every time they shared the bread and wine in memory of him.

We remember this Last Supper every time we go to Mass and share in the Eucharist. The priest takes the host (bread) and the cup of wine, blesses them, and then shares them with the people in memory of Jesus and his love for us.

JESUS AND THE DISCIPLES AT THE LAST SUPPER.

The *Catechism of the Catholic Church* teaches us that the Last Supper was also the moment when the Sacrament of Holy Orders (priesthood) began. Jesus told the apostles, "Do this in remembrance of me" (Luke 22:19), then said they were to celebrate the Eucharist with God's people.

25 Questions... About the Bible

> Catholics call the week leading up to Jesus' crucifixion **Holy Week**. Holy Week ends with the joyful celebration of Easter, when Jesus rose from the dead.

20

Why did the authorities crucify Jesus?

Both Jewish and Roman authorities were involved in the arrest, trial and crucifixion of Jesus. Some of these people were afraid of the influence that Jesus had over the people of Jerusalem, because they didn't want him to have more power than they did. Even before he came to Jerusalem for the last time, he had become known as a miracle worker and an inspiring teacher. After he entered the city to cheering crowds, some religious leaders became more alarmed at his influence.

Jewish religious leaders in Jerusalem called **Sadducees** paid even more attention after he created a disturbance in the **Temple**. Some people were making money by selling things such as animals for Temple sacrifices. Jesus found that their actions showed a lack of respect for a place dedicated to worshipping God. He turned over the sellers' tables and told them they had violated the Temple. His actions angered the Sadducees and the people who followed them. When he was arrested and put on trial by the Jewish authorities, he was charged with **blasphemy** (doing things that are disrespectful to God), because he claimed to be God's Son. The Sadducees had no authority to put him to death, so they handed him over to the Jewish ruler, Herod Antipas. Herod sent him to the Roman military, which was occupying Jerusalem at that time. Even though he did not think Jesus was guilty, Pontius Pilate agreed to have Jesus crucified to satisfy the crowds.

In the past, some people said that the Jewish people were responsible for the crucifixion of Jesus. Others have used this argument as an excuse for hateful behaviour towards Jews. The Church teaches that this view is wrong for two main reasons: 1) Jesus and his followers were Jewish. Persecuting someone for being Jewish would mean that Jesus, Mary and the apostles also deserved to be persecuted. 2) Both Romans and Jewish people took part in the decision to crucify Jesus. There is no persecution of people from Rome or Italy for this reason, so why single out Jewish people?

Human nature can lead us to fear, discriminate and hate others, especially those who seem different from us. It is these human weaknesses, which all people share, that crucified Jesus. Jesus came to teach us that we can overcome these faults with God's love.

What happened on the first Easter?

Let's look to Luke's Gospel to answer this question. Jesus was crucified on Good Friday. Saturday was the **Sabbath**, a day of rest when no work was performed. It wasn't until Sunday morning that some women who were followers of Jesus, including Mary Magdalene, went to the tomb to put spices on the body (this was a Jewish burial custom). They didn't find Jesus' body, but instead saw two men wearing brilliant white clothing. These men told the women that Jesus had risen from dead. The women rushed to tell the other disciples what had happened. They scoffed at the women, but went to the tomb to see if there was any truth in their story. Peter was the first to arrive. He found the white burial cloth of Jesus in the tomb, but not Jesus' body. He was amazed.

Later that day, the risen Christ appeared to two followers who were walking to a nearby village called Emmaus. It wasn't until he broke bread with them at a meal that they recognized him. (Does this remind you of the Mass? The priest breaks the host at Mass, helping us to see Jesus Christ in the Eucharist.)

25 Questions... About the Bible

THE STONE HAD BEEN ROLLED AWAY AND THE TOMB WAS EMPTY.
GOD HAD RAISED JESUS TO NEW LIFE! ALLELUIA!

Jesus also appeared to the disciples in Jerusalem. They were afraid and confused. How could anyone rise from the dead? He proved he was real by showing them his wounds from the crucifixion and eating a piece of boiled fish.

- In John's Gospel, Thomas doesn't believe the other disciples when they say Jesus appeared to them until he could touch Jesus' wounds himself. That's where we get the expression "a doubting Thomas," to describe someone who cannot be convinced of something without seeing for themselves.

- Good Friday seems like a strange name to use to remember the crucifixion of Jesus. The day probably gets its name from an older term that means "God's Friday."

25 Questions... About the Bible

What happened at Pentecost?

Forty days after Easter, Jesus Christ ascended or rose up into heaven in an event called the **Ascension**. The followers of Jesus felt abandoned. Who would lead them now? But at the Last Supper, the Gospel of John tells us, Jesus had promised to send the Holy Spirit to be with them and guide them. During the feast of Pentecost, 50 days after Easter, something amazing happened!

The twelve disciples (Judas, who betrayed Jesus, was replaced by Matthias as one of the twelve) and Mary, the mother of Jesus, were gathered in what has become known as the "Upper Room" in Jerusalem. They were hiding because they were afraid that people might try to harm them for being followers of Jesus.

Suddenly, they heard a loud wind, and tongues of fire appeared over each person's head. They had received the gift of the Holy Spirit! Now they could begin to make sense of Jesus' teaching and discover the meaning of his life, death and resurrection. They also received the ability to speak in a way that people who spoke other languages could understand them.

At the Last Supper, Jesus told the disciples to continue the work he had begun. At Pentecost, they were given the gift of the Holy Spirit to spread the good news of God's love to others. The Last Supper and Pentecost are the events where the disciples (followers of Jesus) become apostles (leaders of the new community).

> You can read about the first Pentecost in chapter 2 of the Acts of the Apostles.

> The sacrament of Confirmation, when people receive the gift of the Holy Spirit, refers to Pentecost a number of times.

How did the early Church continue the work of Jesus?

The Book of the Acts of the Apostles and the letters of leaders such as St. Paul tell us how the early Christians spread the Gospel message. One of their first concerns was to take care of members of the Christian community. Early Christians were in danger of being killed or put in prison for their beliefs. Stephen, an early leader, was killed by stoning. Paul was imprisoned. Caring for community meant looking after the poor, too. Christians also built up their community by praying and worshipping together.

The apostles and other early Christians continued to share the powerful teachings of Jesus. Many apostles tried to convince other Jewish people that Jesus Christ was the Messiah. James was the leader of the Christian community in Jerusalem. He thought Christians needed to focus their efforts in the Holy Land. Others, including Peter and Paul, spread the message of Jesus to non-Jewish people called **Gentiles**. Christians spread out through the Roman Empire, teaching the Gospel in Greek and other languages. They showed that they believed what they taught by doing acts of charity for those in need. Often, they paid for their beliefs with their lives.

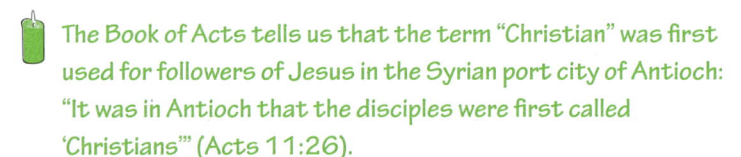

ST. PETER AND ST. PAUL

> The Book of Acts tells us that the term "Christian" was first used for followers of Jesus in the Syrian port city of Antioch: "It was in Antioch that the disciples were first called 'Christians'" (Acts 11:26).

> People who die for their faith are called **martyrs**.

25 Questions... About the Bible

How did St. Paul influence Christianity?

Saul of Tarsus was passionate about his Jewish faith. He saw the early followers of Jesus as enemies. He even assisted at the stoning of Stephen. On his way to **Damascus** to persecute more Christians, Saul had a vision of the risen Christ. This vision led him to embrace the Christian faith. He spread his message to Jewish communities around the eastern Mediterranean Sea, but also to the Gentiles.

Paul was a very gifted teacher. He spoke to many non-Jewish Greek speakers in countries west of the Holy Land, convincing them to become Christian. He used words and ideas his audiences could understand to introduce them to Christ. Paul wrote letters called **epistles** to the communities he had set up in Rome, Corinth, Ephesus and other places. Many of the letters he wrote are in the Bible. For example, his letters to the people of Corinth are found as 1 and 2 Corinthians in the New Testament. Parts of the New Testament letters are proclaimed at Mass every Sunday, and are still helpful for those who follow Christ today.

Paul soon was seen as an influential leader in the early Church. It is believed that Paul was martyred in Rome.

> From June 2008 until June 2009, the Roman Catholic Church celebrated the Year of St. Paul because of his great influence on our faith.

25

What is the Book of Revelation?

The last book of the Christian Bible is the Book of Revelation. If you read this biblical book, you will see that it sounds very different from the Gospels, the Acts of the Apostles and the epistles. It seems to be a prediction of a future with Christ, Mary and the heavens triumphing over Satan, various beasts and hell.

The author identifies himself as John of Patmos. Patmos is a Greek island near the Turkish coast. John received a series of visions that are recorded in the Book of Revelation, which was written during a time of great persecution of Christians. The Christian communities needed support and comfort during these hard times. The underlying message of Revelation is that Christ and Christianity would thrive after a period of great turmoil.

Revelation is written in a kind of code for Christians. It uses numbers to describe figures as evil or good. The main

25 Questions... About the Bible

enemy of Christ has the numbers 666 showing on his head. The number six is seen as a number that is incomplete or bad. The more sixes, the worse things are. As we saw in Question 9, about the seven days of creation, the number seven stands for perfection or completion. The number seven appears 24 times in Revelation. The book ends with a vision of a renewed heaven and earth, to which Christ will return.

> Revelation includes an account of a final battle between good and evil. It says that 144 000 will be saved. This is not meant to be taken literally. It is another code. The number 144 equals 12 times 12. There are 12 tribes of Israel, who are the people of God. The passage is saying that all of God's people will be saved at the end of time. (See Revelation 14:6.)

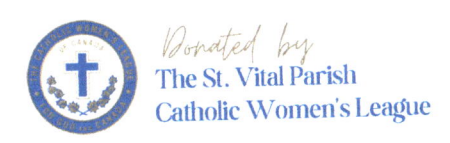

ANOTHER SYMBOL IN THE BOOK OF REVELATION IS THE LAMB. IT IS THE MOST IMPORTANT SYMBOL FOR CHRIST IN THAT BOOK.

Donated by
The St. Vital Parish
Catholic Women's League

25 Questions... About the Bible

WORDS TO KNOW

Annunciation: The Angel Gabriel announced to Mary that she would give birth to the Son of God, Jesus.

Ascension: Forty days after the resurrection, Christ ascended (went up) into heaven to be at God's right hand.

Beatitudes: Eight statements Jesus made during the Sermon on the Mount that sum up what it means to live a Christian life. Some people call them the "be attitudes" for that reason.

Blasphemy: Disrespect for God, Jesus, the Holy Spirit or other holy things or people.

Covenant: A solemn agreement between two people. In the Bible, covenants are agreements between God and God's people, where God promises to care for the people and they promise to live as God asks.

Epistles: Writings in the form of letters, such as the letters from St. Paul and other writers in the New Testament.

Exile: Being prevented from returning to one's own country. The Jewish people were exiled in Babylon for many years.

Exodus: The Israelites' escape from Egypt. "Exodus" is also the name of the second book of the Bible, which tells the Exodus story.

Gentiles: People of biblical times who were not Jewish.

Hebrew: The language of the Israelites, in which much of the Old Testament was written.

Holy Land: The land that Abraham and his descendants settled. It has also been known as Canaan, Palestine and Israel.

Holy Week: The week leading up to Easter Sunday. During Holy Week, we remember the Last Supper, the trial, crucifixion and burial of Jesus, and his rising from the dead.

Inspiration: God's Spirit flowing through the Bible.

Israelites: The descendants of Jacob, who was the grandson of Abraham.

Judges: The leaders of the Israelites after the Exodus, once they were back in their homeland.

Latin: The language the Romans spoke. It became the official language of the Roman Catholic Church.

Lectionary: The book of readings from the Bible that are used at Mass.

Martyr: A person who dies for his or her faith.

Mecca: The holy city of the Muslim people. They believe that Abraham built a shrine to God there.

Muslims: Followers of the religion of Islam.

Nativity: The birth of Jesus.

Orthodox Christianity: A family of Churches in the Eastern world that separated from the Western Churches (including the Roman Catholic Church) in the 11th century. Many of them are found in Eastern Europe, the Middle East and northeast Africa.

Papyrus: The material on which many of the first books of the Bible were written. It was an early form of paper made from the papyrus plant.

Parable: A story used to teach a spiritual truth.

Patriarchy: A system of social organization in which males hold most of the power.

Philistines: A rival group of people to the Israelites. They lived in the coastal area of the Holy Land in the centuries after the Exodus.

Promised Land: The name the Israelites gave to the Holy Land.

Sabbath: A day of rest and prayer.

Sadducees: A powerful religious group in Jerusalem that was opposed to Jesus.

Synagogue: A place where Jewish people gather to worship and study.

Tanakh: The Scriptures recognized by followers of Judaism. The name "Tanakh" comes from the Hebrew initials for the three main sections: the Torah (Law), Nevi'im (Prophets), and Ketuvim (Writings). These Scriptures are almost the same as the Christian Old Testament.

Temple: The sacred place of worship that King Solomon built in Jerusalem. It was later destroyed and rebuilt. The Romans destroyed it again in 70 AD.

Torah: The first five books of the Bible. It is also known as the Law.

Visitation: Mary's meeting with her cousin Elizabeth when they were both awaiting the births of their sons, Jesus and John the Baptist.